Scientific Consultant:
Joseph Peters
American Museum of Natural History

Photo credits:

Breck P. Kent — Cover; Pages 6, 8-9, 11-14, 16-17, 19, 22, 25-26, 28
Wendell E. Wilson — Pages 6, 16-17, 19-24
William E. Ferguson — Cover; Pages 7, 14-15, 17, 27-28
E.R. Degginger — Pages 9, 12, 15, 19, 21-23, 26
Tino Hammid — Pages 20, 24-25, 27, 29
Jeff Scovil — Pages 21, 26-27
Michael Giudice — Pages 11, 14, 28-29
Wayne and Karen Brown — Page 28
Dominick Baccollo — Page 11
J.G. Edmanson/International Stock — Page 8
Oliver Massart/International Stock — Page 10
Roberto Arakaki/International Stock — Page 11
Stirling/International Stock — Page 15
Warren Faidley/International Stock — Page 18
Frank Grant/International Stock — Page 18
Floyd Holdman/International Stock — Page 23
John Michael/International Stock — Page 25
Gamma Liaison — Page 17, 24
Bartholomew/Gamma Liaison — Page 29
Werner Krutein/Gamma Liaison — Page 7
Hoa-Qui/Gamma Liaison — Page 8
G.Brad Lewis/Gamma Liaison — Pages 11, 14
Richard Shock/Gamma Liaison — Page 13
Philippe Hurlin/Gamma Liaison — Page 15
Steve Morgan/Gamma Liaison — Page 19
Bob Schatz/Gamma Liaison — Page 21
Shahn Kermani/Gamma Liaison — Page 23
AP/Wide World Photo — Pages 7, 10, 17, 19

Illustrations:
Howard S. Friedman — Pages 6, 23, 27

EYES ON ADVENTURE™

EXPLORING
EARTH'S TREASURES

Written by
Donald Olson

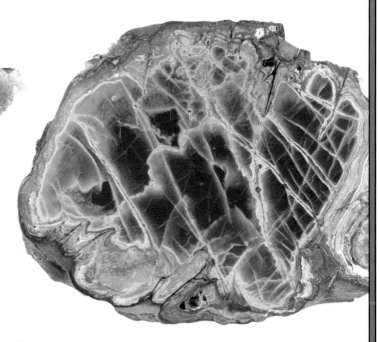

kidsbooks®
Incorporated

PLANET EARTH

From his moon-bound spaceship, the astronaut Neil Armstrong described Planet Earth as "a beautiful jewel in space." This beautiful jewel on which we live is about 4.6 billion years old, has a diameter of 7,926 miles, and measures 24,901 miles around at the equator, its thickest part.

HARD ROCK

If you look at pictures taken from space, you may think of the Earth as a planet covered mostly by water. It's true that water is one of Earth's unique characteristics compared to other planets. But have you ever wondered what's below the oceans and the soil of the continents? A crust of hard rock, ranging from 4 to 44 miles thick.

HOT, HOT, HOT

The Earth is made up of four layers that get hotter the deeper they go. Under the crust is the mantle, which is solid rock topped with molten, or liquid, rock called magma. Beneath the mantle is a layer of fiery liquid metals, called the outer core. The inner core is a solid ball of nickel and iron, estimated to be over 7,000°F.

Snowflake obsidian

A watermelon tourmaline gem set with diamonds.

NATURAL TREASURES

Rich in natural resources, Earth is a treasure box of rocks, minerals, gems, and crystals. These materials are formed by processes above and below the surface of the Earth.

The mineral variscite.

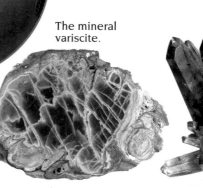
Amethyst crystals

SMOOTH MOVE

Though you can't feel it, except during an earthquake, the crust of the Earth is constantly changing. That's because the crust is not solid but is made up of *tectonic* plates that move. During this movement, the rocky crust gets pushed up, causing mountains to form or grow.

A geologist at work.

▲ Earth's highest mountain range, the Himalayas, were formed about 45 million years ago when two tectonic plates collided and the seafloor between them buckled up.

◀ ROCK HOUNDS

Geologists are people who study the Earth's rocky crust. Rocks, for them, are like pages from a living history book, providing information on how the Earth was formed. Scientists who study how, when, and why rocks were formed are called petrologists. Scientists who study minerals are known as mineralogists.

ERUPTION!

Volcanic mountains are made when one plate sinks beneath the other and red-hot magma is forced up through cracks in the Earth's surface. In this fiery liquid you can imagine the extreme temperatures and forces below the crust. Volcanic action is one force responsible for the formation of rocks and minerals.

A lava fountain in Hawaii.

7

THE BIRTH OF ROCKS AND MINERALS

Our planet is rich with life—millions of animals and thousands of plants. But there is also a wealth of nonliving things. Rocks and minerals are *inorganic*—not usually formed by plants or animals. There are over 3,600 minerals and more than a hundred types of rocks, made naturally by the Earth.

▶ Rocks are made from one or more kinds of minerals. The Dolomite Alps, in Italy, are made of a rock that consists of only one mineral—dolomite.

▲ Salt workers in Thailand.

FOOD FOR THOUGHT

Minerals may not be organic, but there are some minerals that you eat. You shake out one kind over your food. That's right! Common table salt, a valuable resource, is a mineral, and it's mined.

▼ IT'S A HARD ROCK LIFE

Rocks have a life cycle. They change and transform. Fro molten material, sometimes spewed from volcanoes, *igneo rocks* are formed. Worn down by the forces of erosion—win rain, frost, and ice—these rocks break up into smaller ar smaller pieces, called *sediments*, which are deposited in rive or the ocean. As layers of sediment build up, they form new, *sedimentary rocks*. Rocks can also be transformed by heat and pressure inside the Earth and become *metamorphic rocks*.

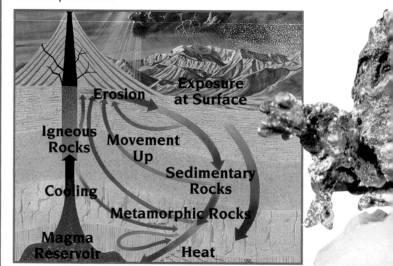

Erosion
Exposure at Surface
Igneous Rocks
Movement Up
Sedimentary Rocks
Cooling
Metamorphic Rocks
Magma Reservoir
Heat

▼ JUST FOR DECORATION

Certain rocks and minerals make beautiful decorative objects. Rocks are tumbled and polished. Minerals are cut into gemstones for jewelry. One very popular mineral is agate. Found in volcanic rocks, these stripy stones are often sliced, dyed, polished and displayed.

Gypsum roses

FANTASTIC FORMS

Minerals form some incredible shapes. They may start out dissolved in air or in water, but over time, heat and pressure turn them into solid matter with a crystalline structure. This process is called *crystallization*. With desert rose, leaflike crystals form when ground water in the desert evaporates, and the minerals gypsum and barite crystallize.

Barite roses

MINERAL CREATION

You've heard that gold is found in "veins." But minerals are not just formed in the cracks of rocks. They come from the fires of volcanoes, crystallize in granite rocks, solidify out of evaporating water, and arise from severe forces of heat and pressure within the Earth.

MICRO ART ▼

Maybe you don't think of science as a colorful business. Well, think again! This lovely picture is a photomicrograph (foe-tuh-MIE-cruh-graf). It was taken after slicing a specimen and viewing it under a high-powered microscope. The picture reveals much about the crystals that lie within.

VOLCANIC ACTION

An erupting volcano is a spectacular and frightening sight. When red-hot liquid magma finds a weak spot in the Earth's crust, it comes spewing out above the surface, hurling lava, ash, and rocks called volcanic bombs.

In 1980, Mt. St. Helen's, a volcanic mountain in the state of Washington, literally blew its top.

LAVA ▼

The fiery magma that rushes out the throat or escapes through side vents in a volcano is called lava. If thick and sticky, it can build up a cone-shaped mountain as it quickly cools and solidifies on the Earth's surface. If thin and runny, the lava flows farther, at speeds of more than 360 miles per hour. It cools and hardens more slowly, creating lower mounds called shield volcanoes.

▲ RING OF FIRE

Most volcanoes are found where the Earth's crust is thinnest, at the edges of tectonic plates or in the middle of oceans. In an area around the Pacific Ocean known as the Ring of Fire, there is a great deal of volcanic activity.

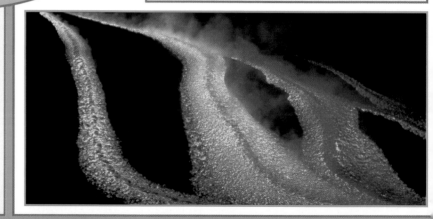

EXTRUSIVE ROCKS

Rocks formed from lava are called *igneous*, which means fiery. If the lava quickly cools and hardens on the Earth's surface, the rocks are said to be *extrusive*.

NATURAL GLASS ▶

Obsidian, a natural glass, is a shiny black extrusive rock. Because it breaks easily into sharp-edged pieces, early humans used it to make hunting tools.

◀ COOL COLUMNS

Basalt is the most common extrusive rock. When basaltic lava cools, it sometimes splits into columns, like these at Giant's Causeway in Northern Ireland.

INTRUSIVE ROCKS

Igneous rocks that solidify inside the Earth's crust are called *intrusive*. They contain crystallized minerals that give the rocks a granular texture and color.

▼ Scientists called *volcanologists* cross the ropy surface of hard lava to learn more about the mysteries within our Earth.

GRAVESTONE

The most common intrusive rock of the Earth's outermost crust, granite is found in many parts of the world. This stone varies in color according to the minerals it contains. A hard and heavy stone, slabs of granite are used to cover buildings, pave walkways, or make gravestones.

Granite

THE PHARAOH'S GIFT

Serpentine is a fine-grained intrusive rock. This stone was quite valuable to ancient Egyptians. Like alabaster and other soft stones used for carving, serpentine belonged to the pharaoh, or king. No one could use these materials unless the pharaoh gave the stones to them.

Serpentine

BREAKDOWN

How do you get sedimentary rocks? Erosion wears at the surface of rocks, and then wind and rain carry the sediments to new locations, often to the sea or to riverbeds. Over millions of years, layers of sediment become buried, one on top of the next. The weight of the upper layer presses down on the lower layers and cements them together into sedimentary rocks.

◀ One of the world's greatest natural wonders, the Grand Canyon in Arizona, was formed by the erosion of two different sedimentary rocks—red sandstone and limestone.

MIRACLE MUD ▼
You may call it mud, but clay is a sediment full of minerals. Found near water, often in the banks of streams and rivers, clay may be gray, black, white, or yellowish. When it's wet, it feels sticky. But when it's packed together, the water gets forced out and clay eventually forms hard rocks called mudstone or shale.

SANDSTONE ▲
Sandstone is a gritty rock composed of layers of sand grains that are firmly pressed together. Because sandstone is fairly soft, it is easily carved. Native Americans in the Southwest carved dwellings out of sandstone cliffs.

▲ PUDDING STONES
Conglomerate rocks are sometimes called pudding stones, but you wouldn't want to sink your teeth into one! A conglomerate is formed when various rocks and pebbles are buried and become cemented together. Pudding stones are often found at the seashore or in riverbeds.

CAVE CARVING

Dark, eerie caverns and tunnels are hidden beneath limestone mountains. That's because limestone, a sedimentary rock, is *porous*—meaning it's full of tiny holes and cracks that allow water to pass through. Over thousands of years, weakly acidic water dripping through makes the cracks wider and carves out caves and tunnels in the soft limestone.

◀ Carlsbad Caverns in Arizona. ▶

▼ EARTHENWARE

Artisans began shaping clay into eating vessels, storage containers, and art objects thousands of years ago. When fired, or dried out, clay becomes hard and its surface can be painted.

SPELUNK IT!

Entering a cave is a fascinating adventure. A cave is full of weird rocks called *stalactites*, which hang from the ceiling and walls, and *stalagmites*, which form on the floor. Scientists who study caves are called speleologists. Other people who explore caves are called spelunkers.

◀ These two spelunkers are exploring the biggest cave system in the world—Mammoth Caves in Kentucky, which run 347 miles underground.

FOSSIL FIND

Did you know that most fossils are found in sedimentary rocks, such as limestone? The reason is simple. When animals and plants die, they usually decay, but if they happen to fall into water and get covered by sediments, their body may become fossilized. Over time, the sediments surrounding them become stone.

▲ This limestone shows the presence of marine fossils. Egyptians carved limestone into coffins called sarcophagi (sar-KA-fuh-gie), a word that literally means "flesh-eating stone."

Schist, full of recrystallized minerals, comes from shale or mud that has been cooked within the Earth.

ROCK CHANGE

Transformation. That is the secret to *metamorphic* rocks, which are igneous or sedimentary rocks that are pushed back into the Earth and changed by underground heat, or pressure, or both. During mountain-building processes, buried rocks are squeezed, folded, and heated up. The minerals within them then recrystallize and form new minerals.

▼ CAST OF COLORS

Prized for its many rich colors and textures, marble is one of the most beautiful rocks on Earth. Pure marble is white, but different minerals can turn it green, red, yellow, or black. When polished, marble takes on a glossy sheen.

▼ MAGIC MARBLE

What's a good example of metamorphic magic? Marble! This stone, found in mountainous regions throughout the world, is created when sedimentary limestone is exposed to high heat and new crystals of calcite grow within.

◀ WRITING ON THE WALL

Rock isn't used just for building. It's also used for communication. Or it used to be. *Petroglyphs* are a form of writing. They're made by inscribing picture on rock. At Newspaper Rock State Park in Utah you can see such ancient communications.

BUILDING BEAUTY

Centuries ago, people used solid marble to construct magnificent temples, palaces, and monuments. Later, they used pieces of cut, polished marble to add richness to the walls and floors of important buildings.

Built in 447 B.C. as a temple to the ▶ goddess Athena, the Parthenon in Athens, Greece, is made of solid marble.

▲ Slate is so abundant in Wales that the Welsh use it to shingle the roofs of their houses.

▲The sedimentary stone known as shale.

SHALE SQUEEZE

Slate is formed during mountain building, when shale is squeezed so hard that the flaky mineral mica recrystallizes within it. The resulting rock is dark gray and splits easily into thin sheets.

COLLECTING CARRARA

A quarry is a place where slabs of stone are cut out of the sides of mountains. The stone is blasted out or cut with special saws. After it's quarried, marble is shipped around the world. Carrara, the most famous marble in the world, comes from a quarry in Tuscany, Italy.

SOFT STONE

Believe it or not, marble is a "soft" stone. That's why it's used in sculpting. Artists use a chisel and a hammer to chip and carve the stone into the shape they want, then polish it. The 16th-century Italian artist named Michelangelo used marble to sculpt many of his famous works.

An artist polishing a marble sculpture.

LIVING WITH MINERALS

People have used minerals even since prehistoric times. Today, industries depend on them to make products like paper, glass, and chemicals. Minerals are all around you, and they're all very different— in hardness, color, and luster. But there are ways to identify them.

◀ As beautiful as it is, sulfur's smell is not so attractive. It's used to make insecticides.

NOT SO HARD

Hardness is not so hard to test, thanks to Frederick Mohs, a German mineralogist who devised a scratch test in 1822. Mohs selected 10 minerals and assigned them numbers for increasing hardness. By scratching these known minerals with an unknown specimen, you can determine the specimen's relative hardness. The softer mineral will always show the scratch. You can also use some household items to test your specimen.

MOHS'S SCALE	HOUSEHOLD TEST
1. Talc	Scratch with fingernail
2. Gypsum	Scratch with fingernail
3. Calcite	Scratch with penny
4. Fluorite	Scratch with knife
5. Apatite	Scratch with knife
6. Orthoclase	Scratches glass
7. Quartz	Scratches glass
8. Topaz	Scratches glass
9. Corundum	Scratches glass
10. Diamond	Scratches glass

RUBIES ARE RED

Every mineral has certain characteristics that act as clues to help identify it. Color is one clue. If it's red, it might be a ruby, because rubies are always red.

MAGNETIC MINERAL

Ever feel drawn to certain minerals? Metals certainly do, because certain minerals, such as magnetite, are magnetic. Early explorers like Christopher Columbus used compasses made from magnetite when navigating.

▲ Orthoclase has a pearly luster.

LUSTER
The surface of a mineral reflects light. Mineral reflections, called *luster*, or sheen, include dull, glassy, metallic, or pearly.

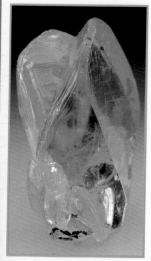

◄ It's not glass, but this mineral has a glassy luster.

SPLIT UP
The way a mineral splits when broken may help identify it. This property is called *cleavage*. Galena (at right) is said to have good cleavage. Minerals that have little or no cleavage are said to have fracture. They sometimes crumble.

◄ Look into this calcite and you'll see double, because calcite's structure splits light into two rays instead of one.

SEE THROUGH
You can see right through some minerals, and they are called *transparent*. But if you can't see through a mineral clearly, it's *translucent*, letting through only some light. O*paque* minerals are the ones you can't see through at all.

◄ This primitive artwork is one of about 300 paintings from a cave discovered in southern France in 1994.

PRIMITIVE PAINT
The first paints ever used were minerals. Primitive artists who decorated the walls of caves ground up minerals from rocks for color. Early Native Americans crushed hematite into a powder and then mixed it with water to create the reddish-brown paint used to decorate their body.

METALLIC WORLD

It's a metallic world. Look around and you'll see the flashy sheen of metallic cars, airplanes, tools, machines, bridges, soda cans, pots and pans. Where does it all come from? Usually, metals are mined from rocks in the Earth's crust. But the process doesn't stop there. These materials need a lot of work to be useful.

MINING ▲

Many ore minerals are first discovered above ground, but then deep shafts and tunnels are dug so that more ore can be extracted. Miners go deep down into the Earth, day after day, to dig out valuable rocks. It's hard and sometimes dangerous work.

Gold is melted and poured into molds to make bars.

ORE STORE

Most useful metals are mined as ore. An ore is a rock that contains a metal, such as copper or gold. Once they're mined, ores must be crushed, separated, and refined.

▲ GOLD BARS ▲

It takes two tons of rock to extract just one ounce of gold. But that one ounce of metal is worth a lot of money. Valued for its beauty and rarity, gold has long been made into precious jewelry and used as a form of currency. People no longer buy things with gold coins, but gold is still made into bars and buried in bank vaults for investment purposes.

PAN IT!

Sometimes grains of gold break free from eroded rocks. The gold may get washed with other sediments down to a river or stream, where fortune hunters swirl the sediments in a water-filled pan to separate gold nuggets from the gravel.

These young panners are searching for gold nuggets.

◀ GOING PLATINUM

Durable, weighty, and glowing with a radiant luster, platinum is more valuable than gold. Although it is put to some very glamorous uses in jewelry, platinum is also used as dental fillings and to reduce pollution from car exhausts.

A bronze statue of Marcus Aurelius, a Roman emperor and philosopher.

PICTURE THIS

In ancient Rome, silver was the more prized of metals. Today it's still valuable, especially where photography is concerned. Unlike gold or platinum, silver tarnishes, or discolors, when exposed to air. Light-sensitive silver salts are, therefore, used to coat camera film. Every time you take a picture you're tarnishing silver.

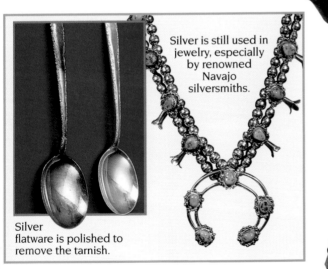

Silver is still used in jewelry, especially by renowned Navajo silversmiths.

Silver flatware is polished to remove the tarnish.

MIXING METALS

The Bronze Age marked an important technological advance for humankind. Around 3000 B.C., it was discovered that adding tin to copper would create a harder metal, called bronze. Such a metal, formed when two or more metals are melted together, is called an alloy. Today, steel is the strongest alloy around. A product of modern times, steel is the skeleton of skyscrapers.

CRYSTAL CLEAR

Crystals are everywhere on Earth. They are diamonds, which can be cut into sparkling gems. They are also the grains of sand on a beach.

▲ A diamond rough and two cut stones.

◄ **SUPER SEVEN**
Growing is what crystals do, and they do it in an orderly fashion. Although there are thousands of crystal shapes in the world, they all fall into seven categories (classes) based on the symmetry, or form, of the crystal.

Cubic-shaped cuprite belongs to the cubic crystal system.

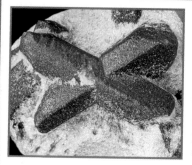

◀ TWO MAKES TWINS

Crystals don't always grow alone. Sometimes two of the same mineral will grow together, forming twinned crystals that look like butterfly wings. Or the two parts can grow into each other, forming a penetration twin, such as a fairy cross (at left).

SPINY HABIT ▶

It may look like a piece of a pine tree, but it's really a crystal known as cuprosklodowskite (COO-pro-skloe-dow-skite). The general shape a crystal takes is called its habit.

With cuprosklodowskite, the habit is needlelike. The needles are fragile, but they're sharp enough to puncture skin.

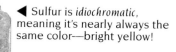

◀ Sulfur is *idiochromatic*, meaning it's nearly always the same color—bright yellow!

BLAZING ▶ COLOR

A crystal can dazzle the eye with its brilliant color. Depending on the impurities present, crystals of a particular mineral can be different colors. Quartz crystals look like glass when they're pure. When an iron impurity is present, you may get citrine, a golden variety of quartz.

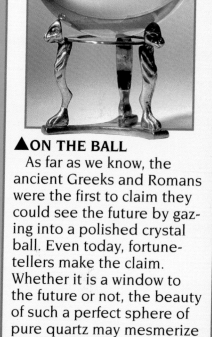

▲ON THE BALL

As far as we know, the ancient Greeks and Romans were the first to claim they could see the future by gazing into a polished crystal ball. Even today, fortune-tellers make the claim. Whether it is a window to the future or not, the beauty of such a perfect sphere of pure quartz may mesmerize even the nonbeliever.

TECHNO-CRYSTALS

Crystals really come in handy. Scientists have discovered that crystals do some pretty amazing things. They've also learned how to grow synthetic, or artificial, crystals in the laboratory. Synthetic crystals such as silicon are an important part of modern technology, used extensively in computers and other electronics.

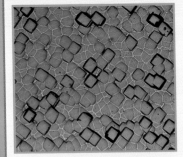

▲ A silicon chip.

GOOD VIBRATIONS

Over a hundred years ago, it was discovered that certain crystals vibrate when they come in contact with an electrical charge. Quartz vibrates more than 30,000 times per second. The pulse is so regular, quartz crystals can be used in watches to tick off time. In fact, there's such a demand for them, they're now made in laboratories.

◀ Quartz

A laboratory-grown ruby.

MAKE YOUR OWN

Once scientists discovered how diamond crystals form, they learned how to grow them in the lab. Today, scientists use a variety of techniques to grow flawless diamonds, rubies, and emeralds.

THE PRESSURE'S ON

Do you know of a crystal valued by the U.S. Navy? Tourmaline is definitely one. It takes on an electrical charge when heated or subjected to changes in pressure. For this reason, the crystal is used in pressure-detecting gauges in submarines.

LASER CUT ▶

Light directed through certain synthetic crystals, such as rubies, becomes a sharp laser beam. A laser can be focused to such a precise spot, its heat cuts through solid matter.

Doctors now use lasers instead of scalpels in some surgical operations.

This diamond is industrial grade.

OUT IN SPACE

Crystals of diamond can withstand even the extreme conditions of outer space. A diamond window in the Pioneer Venus probe allowed pictures to be taken in the scorching atmosphere of Venus.

LAY IT ON ▲

Throughout history, people have believed certain crystals have the power to heal or protect. Today's New Age healers say that crystals placed on the body will increase energy and healing. Crystal healing is sometimes referred to as "the laying on of stones."

CRYSTAL LAB

Growing crystals is something you can do at home. With the help of an adult, you can turn your kitchen into a crystal laboratory. You'll need the following:

1. A jar or plastic cup
2. 3 tablespoons of water
3. 3 tablespoons of liquid laundry bluing
4. 3 tablespoons of salt
5. 1 tablespoon of ammonia
6. A second container, such as a margarine tub or an aluminum pie pan
7. Assorted rocks and a broken piece of charcoal briquette

Mix the water, bluing, salt, and ammonia together in the jar or cup. Then, in the pie pan, arrange the rocks and charcoal briquette. Spoon the solution over the rocks and charcoal. Let it sit undisturbed for at least 24 hours.

You'll be surprised at what you've created.

23

WHAT A GEM!

When you think of treasure, you may think of gems—diamonds, rubies, sapphires, and even garnets. Gemstones are minerals with great ornamental value. That value is determined by their clarity, transparency, color, brilliance, fire (dispersion), and hardness. Beauty and rarity also have something to do with the value of a gem, but beauty, of course, is in the eye of the beholder.

A collection of differently colored garnets.

THE HOPE

Diamonds aren't always clear and colorless. They may be black, pink, yellow . . . or blue, like the famous Hope Diamond. The Hope is 44.52 carats worth of stone, and has been valued at $200,000,000.

DIAMOND FIND

The huge diamond known as the Star of Africa was cut from the largest diamond ever found, the Cullinan crystal, which weighed 3,106 carats. A carat is one-fifth of a gram, or .035 ounces. So, the Cullinan weighed in at one and a half pounds. It was eventually cut into 105 different stones. Two of the largest Cullinan stones now rest in the British imperial state crown.

UNCONQUERABLE

Diamonds are probably the best-known gems in the world, valued for their fire and supreme hardness. The word "diamond" actually comes from the Greek word "adamas," which means "unconquerable."

▲ COLOR FLASH

Although it's important for a gem to be hard enough to be worn every day, some are actually quite fragile. Opal has a tendency to crack and chip, but its flashes of color make it a popular gemstone.

24

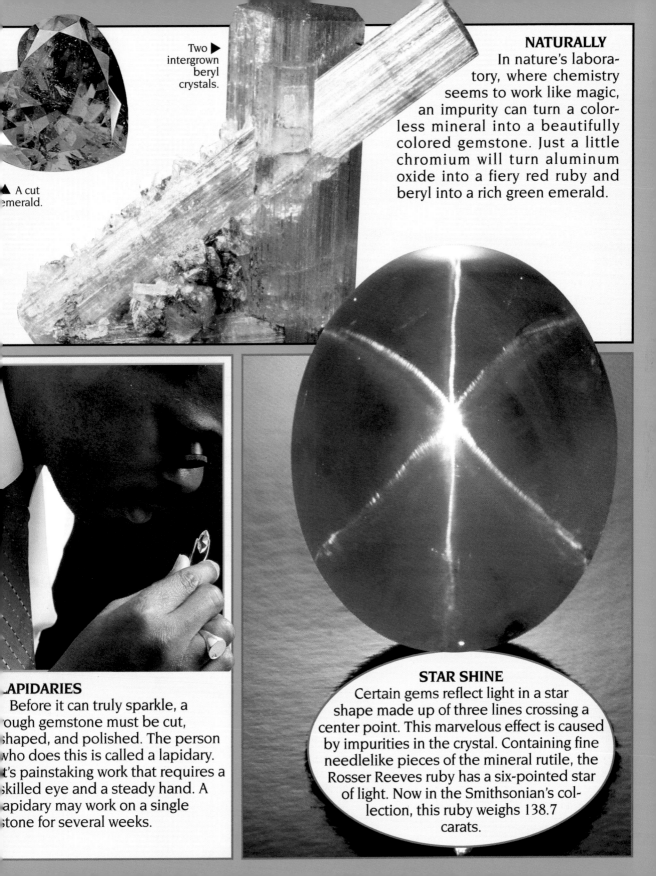

A cut emerald.

Two intergrown beryl crystals.

NATURALLY

In nature's laboratory, where chemistry seems to work like magic, an impurity can turn a colorless mineral into a beautifully colored gemstone. Just a little chromium will turn aluminum oxide into a fiery red ruby and beryl into a rich green emerald.

LAPIDARIES

Before it can truly sparkle, a rough gemstone must be cut, shaped, and polished. The person who does this is called a lapidary. It's painstaking work that requires a skilled eye and a steady hand. A lapidary may work on a single stone for several weeks.

STAR SHINE

Certain gems reflect light in a star shape made up of three lines crossing a center point. This marvelous effect is caused by impurities in the crystal. Containing fine needlelike pieces of the mineral rutile, the Rosser Reeves ruby has a six-pointed star of light. Now in the Smithsonian's collection, this ruby weighs 138.7 carats.

GEMS-A-PLENTY

We tend to think of gems as rare objects. Maybe it's their amazing sparkle or bold colors, combined with the fact that they're made by nature. But gems are all around us, very much a part of our lives and our cultures. Even since prehistoric times, people have sought out objects to ornament their bodies or their homes.

◀ In this perfume bottle, you can see citrine, jade, sapphire, amethyst, and gold.

▲ Petrified wood is a fossil that has long been used to make jewelry.

FOSSIL GEM

Organic gems are derived from once-living plants and animals. The gem known as amber is formed from the sticky sap secreted by pine trees 50 million years ago. Sometimes the ancient body of an insect or other small animal is trapped inside. Used since prehistoric times for jewelry, amber is still a popular gemstone.

▼ A piece of amber with a fossilized insect.

JADE ▶

The ancient Chinese sometimes buried their dead in suits of jade. They believed that this hard gemstone had magical powers and would preserve the dead person's spirit. Jadeite and nephrite are two different minerals, but the opaque gemstones they form are both called jade. We think of jade as green, but it can be many colors.

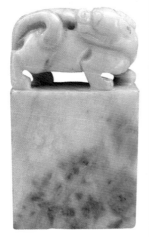

A Chinese carving of jadeite.

◀ TURQUOISE

This stone has been used since ancient times. The Egyptians ornamented mummies with turquoise. Native Americans in the southwestern United States have been carving the opaque blue-green stone into jewelry for thousands of years.

▲ Turquoise in the rough.

◀ BORN OF SAND ▶

Pearls are organic gems that grow when a grain of sand lodges inside an oyster or mussel shell, and the animal surrounds it with a shiny white substance called *nacre*. Pearl divers still scour the deep for these underwater gems, especially in the Persian Gulf and the seas around Malaysia and Australia.

A free-form pearl formed by an Abalone mollusk.

BIRTHSTONES

BIRTHDAY LUCK

There are special gemstones, called *birthstones*, which represent each month in the year. Nobody knows how, why, or where the custom started, but many people believe that wearing their birthstone will bring them good luck.

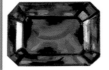

January
Garnet

February
Amethyst

March
Aquamarine

April
Diamond

May
Emerald

June
Pearl

July
Ruby

August
Sardonyx

September
Sapphire

October
Opal

November
Topaz

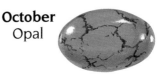

December
Turquoise

27

TREASURE HUNT

The treasures of the Earth are all around you, just waiting to be discovered. If you want to collect them, look around where you live. You may find black, white, and other colored crystals in gravel or sand. Also, contact a local mineral society. They sometimes schedule field trips to nearby areas where you can explore for specimens.

◀ You can get great crystals of pyrite from nature stores or find chunks of this mineral in Arizona and Colorado.

▲ DIRT DETECTIVES

Who knows? If you're an amateur rock hound today, tomorrow you may decide to become a petrologist, geologist, or mineralogist. Also, there are some scientists who combine police work with their study of rocks and minerals. Working for the FBI, these detectives analyze specimens found near crime scenes and try to match them with minerals in the soil found on suspected criminals or on "getaway" cars.

THUNDEREGGS ▲

Geodes, also called thundereggs, look like dull rocks on the outside, but when split open they reveal a sparkling inner surprise. These wonders form when fluids filtering through the rocks crystallize within. Geodes, found in hardened lava, are prized by crystal collectors. The one above is chock-full of amethyst.

FINDING FOSSILS

Fossils tell us about the creatures that lived on Earth millions of years ago. The creature may have been an enormous swamp-dwelling dinosaur, or a small fish or shell in a long-vanished ocean. Fossils of prehistoric teeth, bones, and shells, all found in limestone, are more common than you might expect.

◀ A great white's tooth (far left), and the fossil tooth of its ancestor—the megalodon.

GEM ISLAND ▶

Sri Lanka, an island in the Indian Ocean, is known as "Gem Island" because so many valuable gemstones are found there. During typhoons, the gems are washed down the sides of mountains along with rocks and mud. Gem hunters scoop up the thick mud and strain it through baskets in the hopes of finding valuable stones.

◀ CYBER ART ▲

What can you do with gems besides wear them or sit them on a shelf? With today's computer equipment, pictures of gems can be transformed into incredible science-fiction images. These cyber gems, with their fantastic colors and otherworldly formations, were created from photographs of crystals.